Straight Forward with Science

MATERIALS
AND
PROPERTIES

Peter Riley

W
FRANKLIN WATTS
LONDON•SYDNEY

To my granddaughter, Tabitha Grace.

First published in Great Britain in 2015 by The Watts Publishing Group

HB ISBN 978 1 4451 3544 1
Library ebook ISBN 978 1 4451 3545 8

Dewey classification number: 620.1

Editor: Julia Bird
Designer: Mo Choy Design
Illustrations: Dave Cockburn/Mo Choy Design

Printed in China

Photo acknowledgements: Johnny Adolphson/Shutterstock: 3, 15b. Africa Studio/Shutterstock: 6t, 13tr, 18t, Anteromite/Shutterstock: 14t. AP/PA Photos: 26t. Arvib85/Dreamstime: 19b. R. Ashrafov/Shutterstock: 20b. Aurora Photos/Alamy: 25l. bikeriderlondon/Shutterstock: 22l. Paolo Bona/Shutterstock: 17t. Simon Bratt/ Shutterstock: 5tl, 21b. bubu45/Shutterstock: 26b. Coprid/Shutterstock: 5tr. Crepesoles/Shutterstock: 4bc. cretolamna/Shutterstock: 20tl. Celso Diniz/Shutterstock: 25r, 31. Christopher Elwell/Shutterstock: 20tr. Ilka Erika Szasz-Fabian/Shutterstock: 13bl. Adam Fraise/Shutterstock: 10r. GIPhotostock/SPL: 17bl, 17bc. Richard Griffin/Shutterstock: 20tcl. Stefanina Hill/Shutterstock: 9c. James King Holmes/SPL: 27t, 27b. huyangshu/Shutterstock: 24. Leyla Ismet/Shutterstock: 8b. Brian A Jackson/Shutterstock: 10bl. Lucie Lang/ Shutterstock: 5bl. Neil Lang/Shutterstock: 5br. Alexander Mak/Shutterstock: 16b. maramorosz/Shutterstock: 2, 12r. Monkey Business Images/Shutterstock: 7t. Nitr/Shutterstock: 6b. M.Unal Ozmen/Shutterstock: 20tcr. P.D.T.N.C/Shutterstock: 4c. Photofusion PL/Alamy: 18b. Phototake Inc/Alamy: 19t. PMUK/Shutterstock: 4bl. Leigh Prather/Shutterstock: 12l. Stephen Rees/Shutterstock: 14b. Julia Reschke/Shutterstock: 28c. Nicky Rhodes/Shutterstock: 21t. Shutterbestiole/Dreamstime: 9t. Paul D Smith/Shutterstock: 11. SPL/Alamy: 7bl. stocker1970/Shutterstock: 9b. Thirteen/Shutterstock: 16t. Alistair Wallace/Shutterstock: 20c. Keith Wheatley/ Shutterstock: 23. wiktord/Shutterstock: 15t. Charles D Winters/SPL: 22r.

Franklin Watts
An imprint of
Hachette Children's Group
Part of The Watts Publishing Group
Carmelite House
50 Victoria Embankment
London EC4Y 0DZ

An Hachette UK Company
www.hachette.co.uk

www.franklinwatts.co.uk

FSC
www.fsc.org
MIX
Paper from
responsible sources
FSC® C104740

Contents

Materials around us

There are thousands of different materials and they are found all around us. Clothes are made from wool, cotton and nylon. Homes are made from brick, wood and glass. The Earth is made from rock and the surface of the land is covered with soil and water. Every one of these things – wool, cotton, nylon, brick, wood, glass, rock, soil and water – is a material.

PROPERTIES

Materials have properties. A property is a special feature of a material. One property of wood is that wood is hard. One property of wool is that wool is soft. A material can have other properties. It may be strong or weak, flexible or rigid, magnetic or non-magnetic, transparent or opaque.

▌Steel is magnetic. It is attracted to a magnet.

▌Wood is opaque. Light cannot pass through it.

▌Wool is a heat insulator. It does not allow heat to pass through it (see page 6).

▌ Brick is rigid. It does not bend.

▌ Glass is transparent. Light can pass straight through it.

▌ Rubber is elastic. It can be stretched and squashed, but quickly returns to its normal size.

▌ Plastic is lightweight. This means it has a small weight for its size.

INVESTIGATE
Classify the materials around you into groups such as rigid, flexible, brittle, opaque. Do some materials appear in more than one group?

Conducting heat

Some materials let heat travel through them. They are called conductors of heat. Materials that do not let heat travel through them are called insulators.

CENTRAL HEATING

Metals are good conductors of heat. Radiators in a central heating system are made of metal. Hot water moves from the boiler through the pipes to the radiators. The heat in the water passes quickly through the metal in the radiators and out into the air to heat the room.

▌These gloves are being dried on a central heating radiator because the metal passes heat quickly to them so they dry faster.

▌The metal in this pan conducts heat to fry the egg.

METALS AND PANS

Lots of cooking equipment such as pans are made of metal. The metal lets heat from the stove pass quickly to the food to cook it.

STOPPING HEAT MOVING

Some plastics are heat insulators. They are used to make the handles of pans and electric kettles, among other things. The surface of the handle stays cool enough to hold, even when the pan or kettle is very hot. Wood is also a heat insulator.

KEEPING WARM

Air is an insulator. Some materials trap air inside them. The air turns the material into an insulator too. Wool fibres are wavy and have air spaces between them. A woollen jumper traps a layer of air over your skin. It stops your body heat escaping, and keeps you warm.

❙ The air spaces between the woollen fibres stop heat travelling through the material.

❙ This climber is wearing a number of heat-insulating layers to keep warm in the cold wind. Air is trapped between each layer.

INVESTIGATE

Fill two plastic cups with warm water and wrap a piece of cotton cloth around one cup and a piece of woollen cloth around the other. Which cup of water stays warmer longer? Which material is the better insulator?

Conducting electricity

Many appliances, such as a television or toaster, need electricity. The electricity flows from a supply of electricity to the appliance through a wire. The wire is a conductor of electricity. It lets the current of electricity flow through it. Most materials do not let electricity flow through them. They are called electrical insulators.

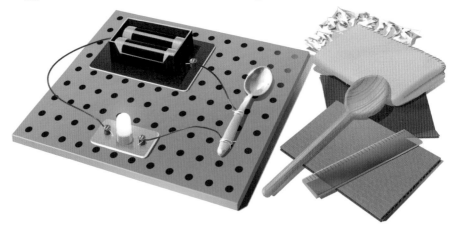

I In this circuit, the lightbulb is on because the metal spoon is an electrical conductor. It would not light up if the spoon were made of wood. A circuit like this one can be used to test materials to find out if they are electrical conductors or electrical insulators.

I Air is normally an insulator, but storm clouds generate so much electricity that it flows through the air as lightning. Water is a good conductor of electricity so stay away from it during thunderstorms!

CONDUCTORS

Metals such as iron, steel, copper and aluminium are electrical conductors. The black material in a pencil, called graphite, is not a metal but it conducts electricity. Water also conducts electricity.

INSULATORS

Wood, plastic and bricks are insulators. Air is usually an insulator too. If it was a conductor, the lightbulb in the circuit above would light up even when there is a gap in the circuit.

INVESTIGATE

Set up the circuit shown on page 8. Test different materials to find out which are conductors and which are insulators.

CONDUCTORS AND INSULATORS IN USE

Conductors and insulators are used together to transport electricity safely from one place to another. Electricity is conducted from plug sockets to appliances by copper wires coated in plastic. The metal takes the electricity along the wire. The plastic coating stops the electricity escaping when the wire touches other objects.

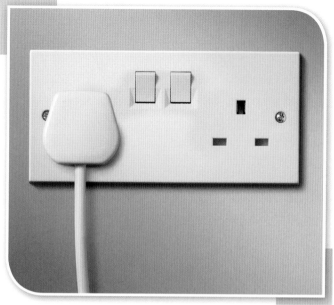

❘ Plugs, leads and switches are all covered in plastic to stop the electricity in the metal reaching your fingers.

❘ Electricity is conducted from power stations along metal cables which are held on metal towers called pylons. Insulating material between the cables and the pylons stops the electricity flowing down the pylons to the ground.

Touching an electric current can kill you. Great care must be taken when handling any electrical equipment.

Using materials

We choose materials to use because they have certain properties. Wood, for example, is used for making chairs because it is strong enough to support your weight, light enough to move around and hard enough to stand up to knocks and scratches.

❙ The wood in this chair is strong, lightweight and hard, yet soft enough to be cut and carved to make attractive shapes in the legs and back.

LOTS OF PROPERTIES

Materials can be combined together so their properties make useful objects. A trainer has soles made of rubber, which is flexible and hard-wearing to protect your feet during exercise. The inside is covered with a fabric which absorbs the moisture of sweat. The outside is covered with a fabric which lets the moisture pass through it so your feet can remain dry. All these materials are held together by a strong glue.

❙ Trainers are made of tough, flexible materials.

BUILDING MATERIALS

The outside of a house is made from a range of materials. Each one has special properties which are used for a particular task.

Roof tiles are made of baked clay and are weather-resistant.

Glass is weather-resistant and transparent. It lets light into a home but keeps out wind and rain.

Bricks are strong and do not break up in rain, wind or frost. They make weather-resistant walls which can support the weight of a roof.

Cement holds the bricks together like glue.

Plastic is lightweight and easily shaped. It is used to make guttering and pipes that carry water to drains.

INVESTIGATE

Scratch some pieces of wood, brick, concrete and plastic which are no longer needed. Which material has the hardest surface?

Solids, liquids and gases

Many of the materials around us are solid materials. There are two other types of materials. They are liquids and gases. All materials can be put into one of these three groups – solids, liquids or gases. The materials in each group have properties that are different from the materials in the other two groups.

A SOLID

A solid material has a definite shape and a definite size or volume. It cannot be squashed to fit into a smaller space. Tiny pieces of solids can flow together like the sand in an hour glass but they do not form drops, unlike liquids.

▌Some solids, such as these minerals, have a crystal shape.

▌Sand may pour through an hour glass like a liquid, but it is a solid because each piece of sand keeps its own shape.

A LIQUID

A liquid does not have a definite shape. It can flow and take up the shape of any container into which it is poured. It also forms drops. A liquid has a definite volume that stays the same, even if you try to squash it.

❚ Liquids can be poured easily from one container to another.

❚ Helium is a gas that is lighter than air. It is used to fill party balloons to make them float upwards.

A GAS

A gas does not have any definite shape or volume. It fills any container into which it is pushed or poured. The volume can be made smaller by squashing the gas into a small container, or larger by releasing the gas into a large container.

INVESTIGATE

Different types of liquid flow at different speeds. Prop up a tray to make a gentle slope and trickle different liquids down it, such as washing-up liquid, honey, oil and water. Compare how slowly or quickly they flow.

Reversible changes

Solid, liquid and gas are known as the states of matter. A material can change from one of these states to another. It can also change back again. These changes in a material's state are known as reversible changes because they can be reversed (changed back).

FROM SOLID TO LIQUID

If a solid is heated strongly enough, it will lose its shape and turn into a liquid. We say it has melted. The temperature at which a solid melts is called its melting point.

❚ This chocolate has reached its melting point and is turning into a liquid.

FROM LIQUID TO GAS

If water is left uncovered, it slowly changes into a gas called water vapour and mixes with the air. This change is called evaporation.

When a liquid is heated strongly enough, some of it turns to gas and forms bubbles. This hot bubbling liquid is called a boiling liquid. The temperature at which a liquid boils is called its boiling point. The invisible gas which escapes from boiling water is called steam.

❚ Most of the water vapour in the air is as a result of evaporation from the seas and oceans. They cover nearly three-quarters of the Earth's surface.

FROM GAS TO LIQUID

If a gas becomes cool enough, it changes into a liquid by a process called condensation. Water vapour in the air condenses when it comes into contact with a cold surface like the inside of a window on a cold day. When steam mixes with air it cools below 100°C and turns into clouds of tiny water droplets.

❙ Water vapour in the room condenses on the cold glass to give it a misty surface. This misty surface is also called condensation.

❙ An icicle starts to form when a water drop hangs from a surface and freezes. The icicle grows as more drops flow onto it and freeze too.

FROM LIQUID TO SOLID

When a liquid has cooled down enough, it turns into a solid in a process called freezing. The point at which a liquid turns into a solid is called the freezing point.

INVESTIGATE

Is there water vapour in your breath? How could you find out?

Mixing

Different materials can be mixed together. The mixture that is formed may have different properties from the materials it is made from.

I This clay and water mixture is being shaped into a jar.

MIXING SOLIDS AND LIQUIDS

Dry clay is made from tiny particles that you can see. Water is made from very tiny particles that you cannot see. When the clay and water are mixed, the clay particles separate and spread out between the water particles. The two materials form a new material that can hold a shape.

DISSOLVING

Sugar and salt are materials that dissolve in water. When a material dissolves it splits up into very tiny particles you cannot see. The particles spread out between the water particles and make the salt or sugar seem to disappear.

I The sugar in this teaspoon dissolves when it mixes with the water.

THE AIR WE BREATHE

Air is a mixture of gases. One of the gases in the mixture is oxygen. We take this gas from the air when we breathe in and use it to stay alive.

Gases from car engines mix with the air. Some of these gases are harmful. If they occur in large amounts in the air, they cause air pollution, which can damage people's health.

❚ When most vehicle engines are working they burn fuel and make gases that pass down an exhaust pipe and into the air.

❚ The suspension of chalk in the water (left) soon settles into a sediment at the bottom of the jar (right).

MATERIALS THAT DON'T MIX

Some materials appear to mix at first, but separate later. When particles of chalk are mixed with water in a jar they form a cloudy suspension. This means that the chalk particles are just hanging in the water. In time the particles settle to the bottom of the jar to form a sediment.

INVESTIGATE

Stir some oil and water together. Can you get them to mix?

Separating materials

Some materials that have been mixed together can be separated again later. Sieving and filtering can be used to separate particles of different sizes. Evaporating can be used to separate water from the materials dissolved in it.

▌The holes in a sieve hold back larger particles, but let smaller particles pass through.

SIEVING

A sieve can be used to separate a mixture of two solid materials which have particles of different sizes. There are holes in a sieve. Material particles that are larger than the holes stay in the sieve. Material particles that are smaller than the holes pass through the sieve.

FILTERING

A mixture of a liquid and a solid that does not dissolve can be separated using a very fine sieve called a filter. Most filters are made of paper that has tiny holes in it. The liquid can squeeze through the holes, but the solid cannot.

▌The mask that this cyclist is wearing has a filter that separates the dust out of the mixture of air and dust that she is breathing.

EVAPORATION

A solid which has been dissolved in water can be separated from the water by evaporation. If the mixture is poured into a dish and left at room temperature, the water evaporates. When it does this, the water particles escape into the air and form water vapour. The solid particles cannot do this and are left behind in the dish.

❚ Water has evaporated from this dish, leaving behind the solids that were dissolved in it. They have formed crystals.

DISTILLATION

Ink is a mixture of water and dissolved colour particles. They can be separated by heating and cooling. The ink is heated in the flask and the water turns to steam. The steam passes along the pipe and cools down. It condenses to water in the pipe which drips out into the beaker.

Cold water flows around the pipe to keep it cool so that the steam condenses into water.

Steam escapes from the boiling water and travels down the pipe.

The water is heated strongly to make it boil.

The coloured particles of ink stay in the flask.

Water collects in the beaker.

REVERSIBLE CHANGES

Separating materials is the opposite or the reverse of mixing them. Separating is a reversible change. Mixing is sometimes a reversible change.

INVESTIGATE

Try sieving some wholemeal flour.
What happens?

Heat and change

Sometimes when materials change they cannot be changed back again. These changes are known as non-reversible changes. When materials and mixtures are heated strongly, non-reversible changes can take place.

BREAD AND YEAST

Most bread is made from flour, water, yeast and sugar. These four ingredients are mixed together to make a dough.

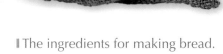
❚ The ingredients for making bread.

❚ This lump of dough is warming in a bread tin whilst the yeast feeds. After baking it will become a loaf of bread (below).

BAKING BREAD

Yeast is a type of fungus which feeds on sugar. When dough is warmed, the yeast feeds quickly and grows. As it feeds the yeast makes carbon dioxide gas. This forms bubbles in the dough and makes it rise. When the dough is baked the yeast is destroyed, the flour is made digestible and the bubbles in the dough expand and make it spongy. This change from dough to bread cannot be reversed.

BURNING

When some materials get hot they burst into flames and burn. They produce carbon dioxide, which escapes into the air. A material called ash is left behind. The black colour in ash is carbon that has not changed to carbon dioxide. The rest of the ash is made from other substances that were in the material. Burning is a non-reversible change.

❚ Ash is left behind when wood burns on an open fire.

FIRING

When clay is heated strongly, its particles stick together to make a hard, brittle material that is used for pottery and bricks. This process is called firing and is a non-reversible change.

INVESTIGATE

Examine some food before it is cooked and make notes about its properties. Look at the food again after it has been cooked. Discover how its properties have changed.

❚ Firing the clay in these bricks has made them strong enough to build walls.

Chemical reactions

Everything is made of chemicals. They may be made of just one chemical like the gas helium in a party balloon. They may be made of two or more chemicals joined together like the gas you breathe out – carbon dioxide – which is made of the chemicals carbon and oxygen.

I The balloon contains just one chemical – helium – but everything around it, including the girl, is made from many different chemicals.

ADDING HEAT

As we have seen, heat can make the chemicals in some substances react together and change the way they are joined up. This change makes a new substance, such as when clay turns into brick. Heat is not needed for some other chemical reactions. These reactions may be fast or slow.

I When baking powder is added to vinegar a chemical reaction takes place that makes lots of fizzy bubbles.

Even in very dry places, moisture in the air leads to metal rusting.

A FAST CHEMICAL REACTION

You can see a fast chemical reaction by combining baking soda with vinegar (see page 22). Baking soda is a white powder made from a combination of the chemicals sodium, hydrogen, carbon and oxygen. Vinegar is a liquid containing the chemicals carbon, hydrogen and oxygen. Chemists call vinegar acetic acid or ethanoic acid. When baking soda and vinegar are mixed together, a reaction takes place between the chemicals in the baking soda and the acetic acid. Some water is made, the sodium dissolves in it and carbon and oxygen from the baking soda form carbon dioxide gas which makes lots of fizzy bubbles in the liquid.

A SLOW CHEMICAL REACTION

Iron is a metal. It can take part in a slow chemical reaction called rusting. This chemical reaction takes place if the metal comes into contact with water. The oxygen from the air dissolves in the water on the metal and reacts with the iron in the metal. The iron and oxygen join to make a chemical called iron oxide. This forms the red/brown flakes we call rust.

INVESTIGATE

Take two wet paper towels and place three iron nails on each one. Wrap up the nails and place one towel in a cold place and one in a warm place. Check each day to make sure they are still wet. After a week open the towels and photograph the nails. Repeat every week for three weeks. Does temperature affect the speed of rusting?

New materials

The world is full of natural materials that we can use, such as wood and stone. By mixing and heating natural materials we can make new materials with new properties.

MIXING METALS

Iron is a metal. It is strong, but brittle. If iron is melted and oxygen is blown through the liquid iron, steel is made. Steel is also strong, but it is not brittle. Steel can be used to make wire, cans and car bodies. Steel rusts when it comes into contact with water (see page 23). If it is mixed with the metals nickel and chromium, stainless steel is made. It does not rust and is often used to make kitchen sinks and cutlery.

▌Liquid steel can be poured into a mould which shapes the metal when it cools down.

I This picture shows a close up of the waterproof fabric Gore-Tex®. It is made from a combination of materials.

KEEPING DRY

Many scientists work at making new materials. The materials have properties which are helpful in special ways. Gore-Tex® is an example of a new material which allows sweat to escape from a jacket without rainwater soaking into it. It allows people to feel more comfortable when they are hiking or climbing.

MATERIALS IN SPACE

New materials have allowed us to explore space. Cermets are materials made from metals and ceramics. They do not break up when they get hot and are used in making spacecraft.

I Lightweight and heat-resistant materials are needed to build spacecraft.

INVESTIGATE

Does waxing a cotton handkerchief with a crayon make it waterproof? How could you find out?

Chemists and new materials

Chemists are scientists who study chemicals and chemical reactions. First they investigate the properties of a chemical, then they investigate how the chemical reacts with other chemicals. These reactions may produce new chemicals. As the chemists make their discoveries, they look at ways the new chemicals can be used to help people.

WASH AND WEAR COTTON

Ruth Benerito (1916–2013) was a research chemist. She investigated ways of stopping cotton fabrics wrinkling after washing. Cotton is made from a chemical called cellulose. It contains carbon and hydrogen linked together like beads in a necklace. Cotton has thousands of 'necklaces' of cellulose, but they are not joined together and this makes the cloth wrinkle up after washing. Ruth worked on reactions between many chemicals and cotton and discovered a way of making the cellulose 'necklaces' stick together. This made the cotton stop wrinkling up after washing. Cotton fabrics with this new property are called 'wash and wear' cotton fabrics. They are often used to make cotton shirts and blouses.

❙ Ruth Benerito won awards for her services to the textile industry.

LESS STICKY GLUE

Spencer Silver is a research chemist who invented a glue with tiny bubbles in it. The bubbles stopped the glue from attaching to things too firmly. and could be reused many times. Another scientist, Art Fry, found the glue could be used on paper to make bookmarks, but more investigations were needed to make the glue leave the surface clean as it was pulled away. Today the glue is used to make Post-it® notes.

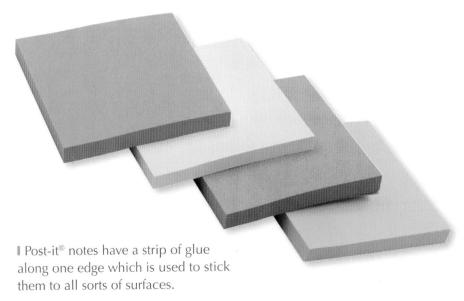

❙ Post-it® notes have a strip of glue along one edge which is used to stick them to all sorts of surfaces.

GRAPHENE

Andre Geim and Konstatin Novoselov are research physicists who discovered the thinnest material ever found – graphene. In 2010 Andre and Konstatin were awarded the Nobel Prize for Physics for their work. Graphene is extremely strong and hard, yet is flexible, transparent and a very good conductor of electricity. In the future, it is expected to be used in a wide range of ways in the production of aeroplanes, computers, cars and solar power devices.

❚ Andre Geim with a model of graphene. It shows how tiny particles of the chemical carbon are linked together to make a thin sheet of graphene.

❚ A graphene transistor. Transistors are used to send electric signals.

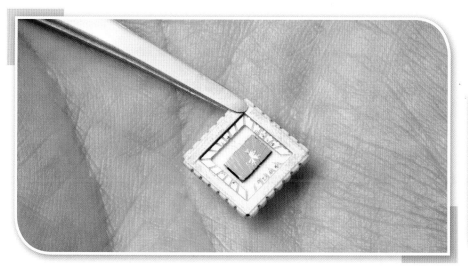

INVESTIGATE

Mix double cream and vinegar and leave for a few hours in a warm place. When you pour it through a sieve, can you see a new material appear?

Particles of matter

Scientists studying matter developed a theory from their observations. They call it the particle theory of matter. It is used to explain the properties of solids, liquids and gases.

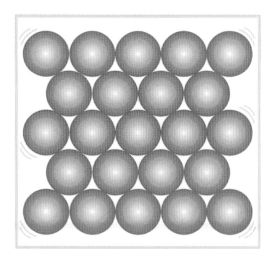

SOLIDS

Solids have particles that hold tightly to each other, as this model shows. This means that a solid always keeps its shape. There is little space between the particles. This also means that solids cannot be compressed (squashed).

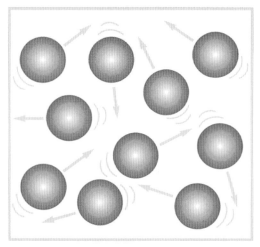

LIQUIDS

Liquids have particles with little space between them. This means that liquids cannot be squashed. The particles do not hold on as tightly to each other as those in solids. This means the particles can slide over each other and a liquid can flow. It also means that a liquid does not have a fixed shape, but takes up the shape of its container.

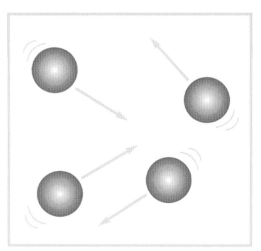

GASES

Gases have particles that do not hold onto each other. This means they are free to move about and they can also have large spaces between them. This means that gases can be squashed. They can also spread out to completely fill a container and not remain at the bottom of it as liquids do.

ELEMENTS

According to the particle theory, all materials are made up of particles called atoms and molecules. There are millions of different materials, but 118 of them have a special structure. They are each made from just one kind of atom which is different from the other 117. These materials with their unique atoms are called elements.

The most common elements on Earth include the gas oxygen, which is in the air we breathe, and the metal iron, which makes up most of the Earth's inner and outer core.

❚ The metal gold is one of the most precious elements.

JOINING ATOMS

The atoms of an element can simply join together to make a material. For example the atoms of iron join together to make a lump of iron metal which we can shape into nails.

In other materials, the atoms of one element can join with the atoms of other elements to form groups called molecules. For example, water is made from molecules containing one atom of oxygen and two atoms of hydrogen.

hydrogen

oxygen   oxygen

❚ The chemical structure of water.

INVESTIGATE

The word 'atom' means indivisible. The idea about materials being made from indivisible particles came from thinking about splitting a material into smaller and smaller pieces. Try tearing up a piece of paper. How small are the pieces? An atom is about a million times smaller.

Glossary

absorb – to take in.

appliance – a device, usually electrical, which is used to perform a task, often in the home.

ash – a grey powder which is a mixture of substances from a material that has been burnt.

atom – the smallest particle of an element.

boiling – a process in which a heated liquid forms bubbles of gas which rise to its surface and escape into the air. Water boils at 100°C (boiling point). It cannot get any hotter. It just turns into steam.

cement – a grey substance used to stick bricks together. It is made from clay and limestone which have been heated together then made into a powder and mixed with water.

ceramic – a material made of baked clay.

condense – the process by which a gas changes into a liquid.

conductor – a material, such as a metal, which lets heat or electricity pass though it.

crystal – a solid material with flat sides arranged at angles to each other. Table salt is a common crystal.

current – the flow of electricity through a conductor.

dissolve – when particles in a liquid become so small that they can no longer be seen.

distillation – a process of separating a solid and a liquid by heating and cooling. The solid is dissolved in the liquid and makes a solution. This is heated and the liquid turns into a gas, leaving the dissolved substance behind as a solid. The gas is then cooled away from the solid and turns back into a liquid.

element – a substance made from one type of atom.

evaporation – the process in which a liquid changes into a gas at any temperature below its boiling point.

fabric – a material made from threads of wool, cotton, nylon or other types of fibre. The threads are woven or knitted together to make a piece of cloth.

fibre – a thin thread.

filter – a material such as paper or cloth which is used to separate very small solid particles from liquids and gases.

flexible – a property of a material which allows it to be bent without breaking.

freezing point – the temperature at which a liquid turns into a solid.

gas – a material which has no fixed shape or volume. It flows and can be compressed.

glass – a hard, brittle, usually transparent substance which is made by heating sand very strongly with limestone and a chemical called soda.

icicle – a long, thin, pointed piece of ice which hangs down, usually from a roof. It forms when dripping water freezes.

insulator – a material, such as thick wool, that does not let heat pass through it, or a material such as pottery or wood which does not let electricity pass through it.

lead – a plastic-coated wire which is used to carry electricity. A lead usually has a plug at both ends. One end will be plugged into a piece of equipment and the other end into a supply of electricity.

liquid – a material which has a fixed volume and can flow. A liquid does not have a fixed shape and cannot be compressed.

melting point – the temperature at which a solid changes into liquid.

molecule – a group of atoms linked together.

opaque – a property of a material, such as stone, which prevents light from passing through it.

particle – an extremely small part of a substance.

property – a particular feature of a material.

radiator – a piece of equipment which gives out heat to warm up a room. It may be filled with hot water from a boiler. The water's heat is lost into the room.

rigid – a property of a material which prevents the material from being bent, squashed or stretched.

sediment – a layer of solid particles which forms at the bottom of a container holding a liquid. The particles do not dissolve in the liquid, but mix with it when the liquid is stirred. Once the liquid stops moving, the particles sink and form the sediment.

sieve – a piece of equipment with holes in it or made from wire netting. A sieve is used for separating solid particles of different sizes such as sand and small stones.

solid – a material which has a fixed shape and volume. A solid cannot be compressed.

spacecraft – a vehicle that travels in space.

steam – the gas that water forms at 100 °C.

steel – a metal made from iron. There are different kinds of steel. They are used for making food cans, car bodies, saws and the metal structure of new houses.

temperature – a measure of the hotness or coldness of a substance. It is measured by using a scale on a thermometer.

transparent – a property of a material, such as glass or water, which lets light pass through it.

volume – the amount of space which is taken up by a material. The volume of a block of wood is found by measuring its length, width and height and multiplying the measurements together.

Index

ABOUT THIS BOOK

This aim of this book is to provide information and enrichment for the topic of Materials in the Upper Key Stage 2 UK Science Curriculum. There are five lines of scientific enquiry. By reading the book readers are making one of them – research using secondary sources. The text is supported by simple investigations the reader can make to experience what has been described. Many of these investigations are simply illustrative to reinforce what has been read and practise observational skills, but the following investigations are also examples of types of scientific enquiry. Grouping and classifying: page 5; Observing over time: pages 17, 19, 21, 23, 27, 29; Comparative or fair test: pages 7, 9, 11, 13, 15, 19, 23, 25.